The Near-Death Experiences of Doctors and Scientists

Doctors and Scientists Go On The Record About God, Heaven, and the Afterlife

By John J. Graden

D1736567

Other Books in the Near-Death Experiences Series

- *Near-Death Experiences of Suicide Survivors*
- *Near-Death Experiences of Children*
- *Near-Death Experiences in Hell*

Legal Disclaimer

unintentional.

First Edition

Near Death Experiences: Doctors and Scientists Go On The Record About God, Heaven, and the Afterlife

ISBN: 978-1932237078

Dedication

Love beyond words and imagination is a common theme in these stories.

I am in love beyond my imagination with my wife, Janet. She and my children, Alexander, and Christopher, have completely redefined love for me. For that, I will be eternally grateful.

Of course, all praise to Jesus Christ.

For behold, I create new heavens and a new earth; And the former things will not be remembered or come to mind.

Isaiah 65:17

New International Version (NIV)

Are We Just Biological Robots?

Does Consciousness Need a Brain to Exist?

What constitutes me or you or all of us? Are we just a biological mass with a brain whose existence ends upon death? Or, are we spiritual beings having a physical experience in preparation for an after-life?

Does our consciousness cease to exist when our brain dies? Is consciousness a product of the brain or is the brain a conduit for consciousness?

Religion and the NDE

From the earliest records of mankind, the predominating belief has been that when we die, we transition into an after-life. Millions of people have reported visiting the other side and returning in a near death experience (NDE).

The first reported NDE was in Plato's The Republic around 380BC. A soldier died and came back to report an experience that shares many of classic NDE elements. More astonishing is the story from the Holy Bible that the apostle Paul may have had an NDE after he was stoned and dragged to the garbage pile in 46 AD as described in Acts 14:20. In Corinthians 12:2:5 he shares his story and some believe it was an NDE he was describing.

Some presume that the NDE experience is spawned from the religious beliefs of the NDEer. As you'll read, religion has no presence in these extraordinary NDEs even though God and Jesus play huge rolls. Religion is a man-made concept and virtually all religions are based centered around preparation for an after-life. However, God and Jesus predate any, religion, and their message of love and compassion has never wavered.

This fact is a source of frustration for many NDE skeptics as religious bias would be a convenient way to dismiss the NDE.

NDEs and the Skeptic

I think healthy skepticism is important and helpful, but many skeptics seem militant in their canned responses at the first mention of an NDE. Often, their dismissive arrogance fuels a closed minded response that is not of their discovery or investigation but a regurgitation of one of their skeptic heroes' sound bites.

Like unruly teenagers dreading a trip with their parents because they claim to know already the destination, many skeptics are not interested in following the truth to where it leads them but are instead canceling the trip altogether. If they looked at the science, they would have to conclude that these experiences are more than lack of oxygen.

A common argument among skeptics is, "If you can't prove it scientifically, it doesn't exist." To that I ask, "Have you ever been in love? Yes? Then prove it."

I think it is the height of audacity to think that all there is to know and understand about life has to be

9

measured under a microscope or brain scanner.

That's why I wanted to profile physicians and scientists who have had an NDE. Virtually every person in this book was a skeptic before his or her NDE. I think they bring an interesting and credible testimony to the discussion.

The NDE and Science

There are decades of scientific study to support the hypothesis that NDEs are real and not of a physiological origin. One of the more recent studies was especially convincing.

344 cardiac patients were resuscitated in one scientific study. Upon recovery, these patients were immediately interviewed about their experience. 62 patients reported having an NDE. This study was conducted in 10 hospitals in the Netherlands and was published in the medical journal The Lancet, v. 358, # 9298.

These patients had a cardiac arrest and were

clinically dead with unconsciousness caused by anoxia or insufficient blood supply to the brain. In other words, they flat-lined. Because the patients were interviewed right after they resuscitation, it was clear their NDEs were not something they made up years after.

As Pin van Lommel, MD, the cardiologist conducting the study says, "Our results show that medical factors cannot account for the occurrence of NDE."

The fact is that we know very little about the brain and the mind. Nor do we know if there is a difference between the two.

Remember, there was a time when science was convinced that bleeding someone was the best way to treat an ailment. In 1633, Galileo was sentenced to life imprisonment for insisting that the earth was not the center of the universe.

We are just beginning to scratch the surface of how the brain works. Personally, if the human brain is not evidence of intelligent design, then I think there is a lot of denial going on among the intellectuals of the skeptic world.

The Limits of Time and Context

There is one constant refrain from NDErs that even our highly educated NDErs of science echo and that is, "There are no words to describe what I experienced or saw."

What these people tell us is limited to the evolution and context of the current time in history. As an illustration, imagine you could transport Alexander the Great from the 335BC to today. You spend a few days flying him around the world ina jet. You take him to see a film in a 3-D cinema. You show him an HD video of the wonders of the world and space. You demonstrate how the entire world is just a click away in a tablet called an iPad. Then you return him back to 335BC.

How would he explain what he experienced? What references could he use that would make any sense to people in his time and place? I can't imagine that he would have any.

Like Alexander the Great, as educated as our ten subjects are they too are all limited by their current time and place context. When you experience a world without time, place or limitations, bringing a description of that experience back to the confines of our time-based current world understandably would leave you at a loss for words.

When highly educated, articulate NDErs struggle to accurately describe the indescribable, it opens the doors for the skeptics to discard and denigrate.

The stories you are about to read are from people of science who bring a rare perspective to the NDE experience. While they are all different in many personal ways, there is a scientifically educated lens these subjects view the world. Pre-NDE, that perspective was narrow and set in stone. Post-NDE it was expanded profoundly.

I hope you enjoy these as much as I have

discovered them.

Note: For the sake of simplicity in this book, I will use, mind, spirit, consciousness, and soul somewhat interchangeably. There is an argument that they are all different, but this book is more about ten amazing stories than the nuance of definition.

Please visit our Facebook page and Like us. Also, keep an eye out for NDE-Suicides, NDE-Hell, NDE-Children at NDEBook.com.

Table of Contents

What Others Are Saying About John Graden's Work

"Your ability to realize your full potential requires that you release your 'mental brakes.' John Graden's excellent book, The Impostor Syndrome shows you how to eliminate self-sabotage on the road to success."

– Brian Tracy – Author, The Way to Wealth

"John Graden is an incredible guest. He combines humor, insight, and enthusiasm in a way that not only grabs listeners' attention, but keeps them engaged as well. I recommend him for any show."

– Sarah Maria, author of Love Your Body, Love Your Life

How to Replace Self-Doubt is a fascinating book that is easy to read with some very good advice for living a more fulfilling life."

– Joe Hyams, Bestselling author of Bogie: The Biography of Humphrey Bogart

"John Graden's insights on the phenomenon of "Imposter Syndrome" are thought provoking and made for an entertaining interview for my radio show."

–Tara Grace Perry, Host of the "Men's Dugout"

"I wanted to thank you for a most inspired hypnosis discussion in my Psychology class. The feedback was enthusiastic from everyone in my class, including the skeptics."

–Doreen Lewis, Psychology Professor, Webster College

"I recently flew from Chicago to Dallas with one of my employees in order to attend a three-hour seminar given by Mr. John Graden. Mr. Graden is an innovator and an established expert in the business field. The presentation Mr. Graden gave was not only informative but inspirational as well. His delivery was informative as well as entertaining. I feel that as a motivator and leadership expert anything Mr. Graden has to say should be listened to. I came away with a whole new perspective of our business and ideas that will help me to become an even better owner."

–Bert Witte, Buffalo Grove, Illinois

"John Graden is in the upper echelon of professional speakers. When he speaks, our clients listen and more importantly, they take action. We have brought him back over and over again, and he never fails to deliver a fresh, funny and invigorating presentation."

– Joe Galea, President, Member Solutions

Foreword

Near-death experiences (NDEs) may be some of the best proof of a power way beyond our physical minds.

Many people in many places have called this power many things. It is the fundamental principle of most religions, philosophies, and metaphysical teachings. It underlies much of psychology and is the cornerstone of all success and achievement.

The first NDE story of this book is that of the great Austrian psychoanalyst, Carl Jung. Jung said that the collective wisdom and knowledge of all the ages is in the collective unconscious and was available to everyone.

Ralph Waldo Emerson referred to it as the "oversoul." He wrote, "We live in the lap of immense intelligence that, when we are in its presence, we realize that it is far beyond our human mind." Emerson, the great American transcendentalist, felt that all power and possibility for the average person came from using this mind on a regular basis.

Napoleon Hill, perhaps the greatest researcher on success of the twentieth century, called this power the "infinite intelligence." After spending more than twenty years interviewing five hundred of the most successful men and women alive in America at that time, he concluded that, without exception, their ability to tap into this higher form of infinite intelligence was the primary reason for their great success in life.

Whatever you choose to call it, this power is as available to you at this very minute as it ever has been to anyone, anywhere. I refer to it as the "super-conscious mind," the mind that is above and outside all other minds or intelligence.

As you'll read in these stories, almost to a person these subjects were highly intelligent and educated people of science. But it wasn't until after their near-death experience that they fully began to understand the power of the super-conscious mind and its existence outside the human brain.

The super-conscious mind is the source of all pure creativity. It is the super-conscious mind that is functioning at the creation of anything that is completely new in the universe. The super-conscious mind was tapped into and used by all the great inventors, writers, artists, and composers of history on a regular basis, right up to the present day. Every great work of art or creativity is infused with super-conscious energy.

Your super-conscious mind can access every piece of information stored in your conscious and subconscious minds. It can also access data and ideas outside your experience because it lies outside your human mind. That is why it is called a form of universal or infinite intelligence.

You will often get ideas that come to you from far beyond you. It's not unusual for two people separated by thousands of miles of distance to come up with the same idea at the same time. When you are well attuned to another person, such as your spouse or mate, you will often have thoughts identical to him or her at the same time during the day, and you will only find out that you had reached the same conclusion when you compare notes hours later. This is an example of your super-conscious mind at work.

Sometimes when you are with other positive, goal-oriented people, your combined super-conscious minds will form a higher mind that you can all tap into. This is why, when you're involved in a conversation or listening to a lecture, ideas and inspirations will often leap into your mind that have no direct connection to what is being discussed. But those ideas and inspirations may be exactly what you need at that moment to move you forward on your journey.

Because of your super-conscious powers, virtually anything that you can hold in your mind on a continuing basis, you can have. Emerson wrote, "A man becomes what he thinks about, most of the time." Earl Nightingale wrote, "You become what you think about." In the Bible, it says that,

"Whatsoever a man soweth, that also shall he reap." And this law of sowing and reaping refers to mental states—to your thoughts.

Of course, there is a potential danger in the use of your super-conscious mind. It is like fire—a wonderful servant, but a terrible master. If you use it improperly and think negative or fearful thoughts, your super-conscious mind will accept your thoughts as a command and go to work to materialize them into your reality. What is the difference between successful people and unsuccessful people? It is as simple as this: Successful people think and talk about what they want, and unsuccessful people talk about what they don't want.

The beauty of learning about these near-death experiences is that we don't have to have one in order to learn the great lessons they teach—lessons about the importance of love, compassion, and that the super-conscious far exceeds the capabilities and confines of the human brain. Best of all, the super-conscious is available to all of us to help us live a more successful, fulfilling, and creative life.

Brian Tracy

BrianTracy.com

Carl Jung

Memories, Dreams, Reflections

"The unconscious psyche believes in life after death." - Carl Jung, M.D.

Of our ten subjects, Carl Jung may end up as the strongest proponent of consciousness outside the confines of the brain.

His idea of the collective unconscious in many ways mirrors the comments and observations of many NDErs who seemed to gain a powerful insight that "all is one and one is all." Jung's concept of the collective unconscious is a reservoir of all the experience and knowledge of the human species.

One of the most influential figures in the history of psychology, Carl Gustav Jung's fascination with medicine and spirituality led him to the field of psychology.

In 1902, he completed his dissertation, "On the Psychology and Pathology of So-Called Occult Phenomena" and graduated from the University of

Basel with a medical degree.

He is renowned for his studies of the collective unconscious, dream analysis, and the human psyche.

Jung believed the human psyche existed in three parts: the ego (the conscious mind), the personal unconscious, and the collective unconscious. Jung believed the collective unconscious was a reservoir of all the experience and knowledge of the human species.

He died in 1961.

The Near-death Experience

In 1944, he had a near-death experience after he broke his foot and had a heart attack while in a Swiss hospital. He provided a vivid description of the experience in his biography, Memories, Dreams, Reflections.

"In a state of unconsciousness, I experienced the variance in visions that must have begun when I hung on the edge of death and was being given oxygen and camphor injections. The images were so tremendous that I concluded that I was close to death."

The Light

This story may have the only near-death experience where a reference to light came from an observer and not the one experiencing the near-death experience. The attending nurse later told Jung, "It was as if you were surrounded by a bright glow."

He felt like he was very high in space floating above the earth, which he described as bathed in a "gloriously blue light."

He saw the sea and recognized the continents and even Ceylon and India, so this was not a different land or an alternate earth or universe that is more common in NDEs.

Afterward, he found out that in order to have a

view like this he would have to be one thousand miles above the earth. The sight of the earth from this height was the most glorious thing he'd ever seen. He also felt he was on the point of departing from the earth.

He turned around and saw a huge block of stone, like a meteorite. It was about the size of a house, or even bigger. The stone was also floating in space.

He saw an entrance in the stone that led to a small room, a room similar to ones he'd seen in Ceylon. A black Hindu in a white gown sat in lotus posture on a stone bench. Jung was sure the Hindu was expecting him.

As he moved toward the entrance, a strange thing happened. He had the feeling that everything he ever aimed at or thought of was being taken ay. Everything fell away or was painfully stripped from him.

The experience gave him a feeling of extreme poverty but, at the same time, great fullness. There was no longer anything he wanted or desired. He existed in an objective form; he was what he experienced. He felt sure that he would finally understand where he fit in the "historical nexus." The rock temple would answer all of the questions of his life.

The Guide

While considering moving into the temple, he saw an image floating up from the earth. It was his doctor but in his primal form. Consistent with NDE guides, the communication was non-verbal or, as Jung put it, mute.

The doctor had been sent to deliver a message to Jung, to tell him that there was a protest against his going away. He had no right to leave the earth and must return. The moment he heard that, the vision ceased.

The Aftermath

Jung was disappointed because he could not enter the temple to join the people and have his questions answered. That disappointment lingered for about three weeks. He said he couldn't make up his mind to live again.

He lamented about being back in the "box system" again. After his experience, he viewed the earthly world as a "three-dimensional world that had been artificially built, in which each person sat by himself in a little box."

He was not too happy with his doctor for bringing him back but, at the same time, he was worried about his doctor's health. He felt that since he had crossed over to his primal form someone was going to die. He was concerned that the doctor would have to die in his place.

Jung was the doctor's last patient when, on April 4, 1944, the doctor died of septicemia.

Memories, Dreams, Reflections

Book Description

Release Date: April 23, 1989

In the spring of 1957, when he was eighty-one years old, C. G. Jung undertook the telling of his life story. At regular intervals, he had conversations with his colleague and friend Aniela Jaffé and collaborated with her in the preparation of the text based on these talks. On occasion, he was moved to write entire chapters of the book in his hand, and he continued to work on the final stages of the manuscript until shortly before his death on June 6, 1961.

Dr. George Ritchie

What Have You Done With Your Life?

George reached out to tap the man on the shoulder, but his hand passed right through him.

A private in the Army during WWII, twenty-year-old George Ritchie died of pneumonia in December 1943. While he was dead for just nine minutes, he had a remarkable NDE that inspired Dr. Raymond Moody to begin to investigate these types of experiences and eventually coin the term near-death experience.

As I read George's book, Return from Tomorrow, I could imagine it as a black and white film starring Jimmy Stewart as George Ritchie. It would be like, It's a Wonderful Life meet Heaven Can Wait.

George had an enthusiasm for serving his country in a time of war and was thrilled that he had been singled out for medical training that would significantly accelerate his ascension as a medical officer. But first, he had to catch the train to get to the medical training facility to begin his new life.

The countdown to making that travel connection provided an urgent undercurrent to his near-death experience story that made it both entertaining and compelling.

As a young recruit in the US Army, George was sent to Camp Barkeley, Texas, for basic training in September 1943. Because George had previous medical training, the army was going to reroute him to the Medical College of Virginia to become a doctor under the Army Specialized Training Program. It was a big honor and George was excited about his December 19th train trip to his hometown of Richmond to start the program.

In early December, he developed a fever and was admitted to the base hospital. Confident he would get out soon, he spent his time in the room mapping out every contingent train schedule that would get him to Richmond on time.

After a few days, George was getting anxious.

He was still stuck in the hospital as the big day approached. He spent more hours working and reworking the possibilities of catching the one final train that would get him there.

On the day before he was to leave, he felt good enough to go see a movie on the base with another patient. Afterward, he set out his clothes and duffle bag, set his alarm for 3 a.m., and attempted to go to sleep. His condition worsened. He staggered out of the room to find a bathroom when an orderly saw him, pulled him into a room, and took his temperature. His fever had jumped to 106. The orderly called for help to carry George back to his room. He was being held up by two orderlies when he starting hearing a strange whirring sound inside his head, and his knees felt like rubber. He began to fall.

The Near-death Experience

In the early hours, George woke up in his hospital bed with a start. After all of his preparation, he couldn't believe the worst-case scenario was happening. He was going to miss his train. He looked around in a panic. None of his stuff was in the room. Worse, this wasn't his room. He jumped out of bed looking around. He turned back towards the bed and was stunned to see another guy in the bed. Someone was in the bed he just got out of!

George ran out into the hallways desperately looking for help. He saw a sergeant and asked him a question, but the sergeant just walked on. He started to run to the outside door, and he was swept up into the night sky. He was flying over the ground away from the camp and towards small towns and, hopefully, the train station.

George could see traffic lights flashing below. He was starting to get confused. What was happening was too much for him. He saw the light of an all-night diner and could make out a man walking towards the diner. George descended to ask the man for directions and some help. The man acted like George didn't exist. As the man opened the diner door, George tried to tap the man on the shoulder, but his hand passed right through him.

Now George was wondering what was going on. He reached out to lean on a power pole guide wire and, again, he passed right through it.

George was clearly not in Kansas anymore. He started to realize that missing his train may not be the most important event happening right then. Maybe his train had left for good.

Starting to suspect that he may be dead, George wanted to find his body. That's not something you hear about in many NDEs. Most of the time, there is little interest in the physical body left behind. Maybe as a soldier and a budding doctor, George wanted some proof for closure.

Still, like a dutiful soldier, George felt getting back to the base would provide some answers or at least some comfort. Almost as soon as he had the thought, he was rocketing back to the camp.

He arrived quickly, but he realized he had a new

problem. George wasn't sure he would recognize his face. It may be hard to imagine as I wrote this in 2013, but in 1943, the mirror is about the only reference you would have to your adult face. How many pictures would a twenty-year-old have of himself? Probably very few and they would be in black and white.

As George couldn't look for his face, he remembered that he was wearing a black onyx oval fraternity ring. Now he was on the hunt for his ring and the body attached to it. He couldn't physically move anything, so he was frantically floating/flying to nearly identical rooms looking at hands.

He wasn't sure if he was back in the same room where all of this started, but he saw a guy with a sheet over his head with his arms on top of the sheet. On the left ring finger was his black onyx oval ring.

George's discovery of his body seemed to have been a threshold instant because the room began to get brighter until it was so bright that he thought that, normally, his retinas would have burned out. Leave it to a doctor-to-be to remember the little things. Things were about to get anything but small.

He realized that the source of the light was a Man. He thought, "That's the Son of Man," and George instantly jumped to attention.

He knew he was in the presence of Jesus Christ but not the kind, gentle Jesus of Bible school. Jesus was the most amazing "totally male being" he'd ever met. Jesus radiated an astonishing love. He was older than time, but he was more modern than anyone else was.

George suddenly realized that Jesus knew everything about him. Everything. He knew his every thought and action from the day he was born. George was humbled to say the least. Like most people, not all of his thoughts were pure or his actions right. Jesus reviewed every event of George's life.

Though they didn't leave the room, the walls became living murals of scenes of George's past.

Many scenes were of people in George's life such as when his parents first met, but the focus was the life of George Ritchie.

There were happy scenes and miserable scenes, many of which originated with him. From schoolyard tussles to nasty arguments and lustful thoughts and desires, George was on display in front of the one person in the universe that he would want to please.

However, George didn't feel like he was being judged. He described it more like an accounting. During each scene, Jesus asked him, "What have you done with your life?" The question was more of a filter than a question. Did George live a good life? Did he treat people well? Did he make good decisions?

George answered that he was an eagle scout, and Jesus replied, "That glorified you."

In the presence of Jesus, there was no hypocrisy. Jesus knew what he was thinking. He couldn't think one thing and say another. Nor could he misunderstand what He meant. Jesus knew everything about George, and He totally accepted him and loved him.

The questions moved to love. Had George loved liked Jesus was loving him? George answered that he didn't know love on that level was possible. Jesus reminded him that He taught us all by the life and death He lived, and that you were to love your neighbor as you loved yourself.

Jesus quickly transported both of them to an over-crowded city with buildings and people hurrying by and passing right through each other.

Murderous men and women argued in eternal loops. Children begged apologies for their suicide to their parents who could not see them. Adults clung to oblivious people pleading for forgiveness. Others were fighting and attempting perverse sexual acts, but no contact was possible, as they were all dead. They just kept repeating the attempted acts.

Jesus told him, "They are suicides, chained to every consequence of their act." Jesus was showing him hell.

There were thousands of scenes, and it would have taken weeks, maybe months, to watch them all, but there was no sense of time. There never is in a near-death experience.

George had the sense Jesus was taking him somewhere higher, a higher plain or place or maybe the Vista was just opening up. George wasn't sure.

The air became more transparent as they ascended when before them when giant buildings in a color-saturated park appeared. George sensed there was a relationship between everything he could see. One thing he was sure of, this was a heck of a lot better than the hellish vision he'd just left. There was an all-encompassing peace about this place, especially compared to "suicide city."

George described any attempt to compare what he saw there to anything on earth as "ridiculous."

Enveloped in the love that permeated the atmosphere was an excitement about learning. It was a cosmic college or university. The vast halls and soaring cathedrals were teeming with genderless beings in loose-flowing, hooded cloaks that were reminiscent of monks, but the beings were not religious.

George saw rooms filled with complex equipment and classes with these hooded figures poring over intricate mathematics and complex chartings. As educated as George was, it was far beyond his understanding.

Jesus led him to a studio where beautiful, complex music was being created and performed. Next, they entered a vast library that he thought must contain the most important books in the universe.

George asked Jesus if these people had grown beyond selfish desires while on earth. Jesus communicated, "They grew, and they have kept on growing."

Understandably, George had many questions, but he began to feel they were incidental. He felt Jesus could only show him what he was capable of understanding.

But, Jesus had more to show him. Jesus took him to a bright, luminous, seemingly endless city. Everything seemed to be made of light. George was in awe. The city seemed light years away but was radiant.

Two beings broke from the city and flew towards them. But, as fast as they approached Jesus took George away even faster.

The light began to fade; the space began to close in, and George was back in his hospital room. Jesus stood next to him, almost to protect him during the transition, or maybe to convince any part of George that may have doubted the experience he just had.

Jesus brought Georges' attention downward. George saw his body below, but he felt nothing about it. Jesus said that part of his purpose was to help return George to his body. George protested, but to no avail, and was returned to the form of what he described as "that lump-like thing" in the bed.

The Aftermath

Like many NDEers, George was left with a lonely longing to return to the presence of Jesus Christ. Who wouldn't? Returning to "regular life" was not easy for George, but his military duties kept him busy. Though he had indeed missed his train, the Army extended his start date, so he entered and struggled somewhat in the Army Specialized Training Program.

Eventually, he completed the program, and he was shipped off to Europe.

In 1945, he was a first responder to a horrific train crash in France. The Vichy French forces under Nazi control switched the train tracks. The train smashed into a brick wall at full speed. The carnage was like nothing he'd ever seen, but he wished he'd been a victim rather than a rescuer. He still felt stuck on the earth and wanted to be back in the "cosmic college" rather than where he was.

The contrast of the love that Jesus showed him and the harsh reality of human hatred enacted on

47

earth stunned him. It was also isolating because he was alone in his near-death experience.

As George assisted with the triage and care, he realized this was his first exposure to human suffering on a large scale. He thought if hatred could grow to be this powerful, who would want to live in this world?

At the end of a nightmare day, he lamented that the dead had been permitted to leave this world while he was condemned to stay. He envied those who had died that day. He longed for death and felt his survival was a judgment on him and rejection from Jesus.

George tended to a sergeant whose knee had been nearly blown off. The man's name was Jack Helms. There was something strongly familiar about Jack. He had a sunburst smile and was deeply interested in other people's lives.

Prior to meeting Jack, George had just put in the hours on his shift; now, he found himself staying late to be around Jack. One day, George told Jack about his NDE. He could tell Jack was fascinated and had no doubt about the truth of his story. As George told the story, he realized that the strange familiar feeling he had with Jack was that Jesus was looking at him out of Jack's eyes. The acceptance and the caring in Jack's eyes were what he recognized, only this time he was on a hillside in France five thousand miles from the camp hospital in Texas.

George realized that his desire to be in the presence of Jesus was misplaced. Jesus is present everywhere. George knew that afternoon after talking with Jack that if he wanted to feel close to Christ he would have to find it in the people that He put in front of him every day.

George learned to look for Jesus in the face of everyone he met. The more he learned to see Christ in others, the less he was affected by the death and suffering he had to deal with every day as a medic. He also began to comprehend that what Jesus showed him was not paradise. That was only half of the journey. The other half was the horrific, savage, violent, sexual, materialistic loops of an eternity in hell.

Towards the end of the war, George witnessed hell on earth. His unit was assigned to bring medical supplies to help the newly liberated prisoners in the concentration camp near Wuppertal. Though he'd seen the carnage of bodies torn apart by explosions, the brutal effects of slow starvation and torture was a new kind of horror. When it became unbearable, George would go from one end of the camp to the other looking into men's faces to find Christ looking back.

In the concentration camp, he found a Polish prisoner nicknamed Wild Bill Cody. Wild Bill had a great energy, bright eyes, and he was fluent in five languages. He was a huge help in sorting out the paperwork to relocate and return the war prisoners to their families or hometowns, many of which had been wiped out.

Wild Bill's compassion for his fellow prisoners

glowed on his face. George was stunned to discover that Wild Bill had been in the concentration camp since 1939—six years of starvation and disease without any physical or mental deterioration!

He was a leader and friend among the prisoners. They turned to him to mediate differences. Many of the nationalities of the prisoners hated each other as much as they hated the Germans. Wild Bill helped to mediate their differences and taught them forgiveness.

Wild Bill walked the talk of forgiveness. When the Germans entered his town of Warsaw in 1939, they took everyone, including his wife and five children, lined them up against a wall, and shot them dead with machine guns. Though he pleaded to die with his family, they made him watch their execution. Then they sent him to a work camp because he could speak German.

After witnessing such a monstrous act, he knew he had to make a choice. He could hate the soldiers.

As a lawyer, he'd seen too often what hate could do to a person's soul and body. He said it was an easy decision. Hate had just killed his family. Hate could not be the answer. Instead, he decided that he would love every person he came into contact with for the rest of his life.

His love kept him alive and well in the face of untold brutality.

Years later, in 1952, George was flipping through an issue of Life magazine when he saw a drawing of the first atomic submarine. That article prompted him to share his NDE story because men were entering the age of atomic power without understanding the creator of the power, God.

He began speaking to groups with a message that everything that was not God was hell. It was a professional risk, but he felt compelled to take that step. In 1978, he co-authored a book with Elizabeth Sherril, called Return from Tomorrow, telling his amazing story. The book sold over two hundred thousand copies. In 1998, he co-authored a book with Ian Stevenson called *Order to Return: My Life After Dying.*

George Ritchie, M.D., passed on October 29, 2007.

Dr. Anthony Cicoria

The Accidental Pianist

That body on the ground was not him.

At a 1994 family reunion in upstate New York, Dr. Anthony Cicoria, an orthopedic surgeon, placed a call from a payphone. While he was talking, he heard a loud crack when a lightning bolt shot through the phone into his face and came out of his foot.

Although it was over in an instant, Anthony felt as though he was moving in slow motion. The shock sent him flying backwards, but then he suddenly stopped and started going forward. What happened next mystifies him to this day.

His mother-in-law screamed and began to run towards him. He was wondering what was going on. She ran right by where he was standing to where he was lying on the ground. Anthony realized that he was dead. His exact thought was, "Oh s***, I'm dead," though he felt no emotion about it.

He could see the lady who was waiting to use the phone after him. Fortuitously, she was a trained emergency medical nurse and started CPR on him. Anthony could see and hear them, but they couldn't see or hear him.

The Near-death Experience

The first realization he had was that he had remained conscious through the experience of transitioning from the physical to the spiritual, so that body on the ground was not him. He was in a spiritual form. His consciousness was with him. His thoughts were with him. Therefore, consciousness must be his true identity.

The second realization was that the experience lacked emotion. He had no emotion associated with the fact that he was dead.

He started floating up the stairs. As he looked down at his legs, he saw that they were starting to dissolve. He was becoming a spirit form. At the top of the stairs, he passed through the wall to see his family. They were all having fun painting faces. He thought, "They'll be fine." He had no emotion about never seeing them again.

He floated out of the building. As he left the building, he was wrapped in a blueish white light. He felt an overwhelming sensation of absolute love and peace. It was like falling in a river of pure positive energy, which he thought was God.

He knew where he was going, and it was not to be feared. In fact, he felt he was being taken someplace good. He didn't know where, but he was very happy about it. He had a brief review of the highlights and lowlights of his life that ended quickly. It was not an in-depth review. As soon as he began to really appreciate the blissful joy he was experiencing, he was reunited with his body and the pain of the burns on his face and foot. It was over.

He was angry. He begged God not to make him return. He went from absolute bliss to burning pain in his head and foot. He wanted the nurse to stop trying to save him. He just wanted to go back to heaven and be with God. His body was still unconscious although he could see, hear, and feel everything.

After a few minutes, the nurse stopped CPR and Anthony opened his eyes, sat up, and thanked her.

The Aftermath

As he survived being hit by lightning, he figured he was fine, so he refused to go to the hospital. Several weeks after the accident, Cicoria consulted a neurologist because he was having difficulty with his memories and was feeling sluggish. The neurological exam, including an EEG and an MRI, found nothing unusual. After a few weeks, his energy returned, and he went back to work. Two weeks later, his memory problems disappeared. His life had apparently returned to normal.

The experience inspired Anthony to research

NDEs. He believed that his consciousness was his identity and that his spirit lived on. We have a memory of how many times we've been on this earth as different beings. Each existence is meant to help you improve as a human being. Using Maslov's Hierarchy of Needs, we all start at the bottom and work towards reaching the top of the pyramid into the state of being self-actualized.

When you finally reach the level of self-actualization, you don't have to return to earth again. You move up in the spirit world.

After his near-death experience, Anthony had an insatiable desire to listen to classical music. That surprised him because he had always been a rocker. He took piano lessons for about a year as a child but lost interest and quit. His desire to listen to classical music evolved into a strong desire to play classical music.

Coincidently, Anthony's babysitter came to him and asked if he would let her store her piano for a year. Anthony took full advantage of having a piano in his house. He would get up at 4:30 a.m. and play on it until 6:30 a.m. before going to work. At night after his kids went to bed, he would play until about midnight.

One night at about 3 a.m., Anthony had a vivid dream of himself wearing a tuxedo and playing the piano at a concert hall in front of an audience. Watching himself play, he came to the realization that the music he was playing was his own. He was able to remember most of the music and started writing his own compositions.

Anthony felt the music and was emotional, and that was important because emotions touched people, and he felt that music was why God had sent him back.

Anthony had also embraced meditation as a way of experiencing the spiritual world and as an avenue to awakening.

Bio

Anthony Cicoria, M.D. (born in 1952), is a doctor specializing in orthopedic medicine, orthopedic surgery, orthotics, prosthetic supplies, and sports medicine. He was profiled in neurologist Oliver Sacks' book Musicophilia: Tales of Music and the Brain (2007).

Audio CD

Notes From an Accidental Pianist, composed by Dr. Tony Cicoria

Dr. George Rodonaia

From Atheist to Ordained Priest

"People who believed in God were idiots."

While most NDEers are dead for up to thirty minutes, Russian atheist and scientist, George Rodonaia, says he was dead for three days. He was run over by the KGB while walking on the sidewalk and pronounced dead at the scene.

In 1976, at the age of twenty, George Rodonaia was a gifted intellect that was already a practicing doctor in the country of Georgia. He never believed in God. He never read the Bible, and he never thought about God or divinity. He thought that people who believed in God were idiots.

Unhappy with the prospects in his country, he attempted to leave his country and move to America. He was also a vocal Soviet dissident during the time when such a stance could get him killed—and it did!

The Murder

On a chilly Friday night, George was waiting for a taxi to take him to the airport to catch a flight to New York when a car suddenly swerved onto the sidewalk and hit him. He flew thirty feet into the air and then the car backed up and ran over him again.

George was pronounced dead at the hospital. Ironically, the doctors who pronounced him dead were his friends in the medical field. Because the death was considered to be politically motivated, George was placed in a freezer in the morgue to allow for an autopsy on Monday morning.

The Near-death Experience

George said he was in total darkness. He was in no pain. He was aware of who he was, but he was in the blackness of a place darker than he had ever imagined. The darkness pressed upon him and terrified him. He had no idea where he was. He went into a mind loop question, "How can I be when

I am not?"

George struggled to gain control of his fear. Why was he in darkness? What was he to do? In an interesting example of awareness during a near-death experience, he recalled the famous line from Descartes' book, "I think; therefore I am." That helped him to settle down and contemplate his situation.

His thought process was that he had to stay positive. He had to resist the pull of panic and a negative outlook in the darkness. As soon as he thought that being positive would bring light it did.

George was immersed in a strong, bright light that he described as a camera flash that never turned off. At first, it was too bright for his eyes. As he adjusted to it, he began to feel warm and comforted.

He began to see molecules, atoms, protons, and neutrons flying around him. He took joy in the symmetry of what seemed like the chaos unfolding in front of him. He saw the universal connection of life and nature. George felt his physical body was a limitation that he happily discarded.

Time no longer existed as he went through his life-review. He saw his life from birth to death all at once. He saw every event in his life but had no regrets or shame for any of them. He was content.

The light continued to radiate a joyful sense of peace to him. He was learning that all the physical limitations of a human life were nothing when compared to this reality. He felt a wholeness and unity with the light, and he felt that everything was connected.

All of time and space was available to him. He had a sudden urge to learn the Bible, so he went back and visited the minds of Jesus and His apostles. He heard their conversations and experienced what they experienced even though he had no body. He was pure consciousness. All communication was non-verbal.

He was deeply enjoying what he was experiencing when he suddenly felt as though someone had grabbed his head and pushed it down. He instantly returned to his body and felt the pain of a scalpel cutting into his abdomen.

His body was cold, and he was shivering. Much to the shock of the doctors, he opened his eyes. They took him to the hospital where he spent nine months in recovery.

The Aftermath

During his near-death experience, if George thought of a location, he was instantly there. When he attempted to communicate with people in these places, he didn't get much of a response, with one exception. His next-door neighbor had a new baby who cried constantly. Nothing they could do would stop the child from crying. They took the child to the doctors, and the doctors couldn't find any way to stop the baby from crying.

George was able to communicate non-verbally with the child. The child communicated to George that his arm hurt. George was able to see that the child had a greenstick fracture in his arm.

Georges' conversation with the baby next door was important because when George told people about his near-death experience, many were dismissive and skeptical. However, when he told his family about the baby next door, the baby was taken to a doctor who discovered that the child indeed had a greenstick fracture in his arm.

George emerged from his experience a completely changed man. Prior to his near-death experience, he was a staunch atheist. Afterward, he firmly believed in God. There is only one God, and that is the God that showed him wondrous stories and lessons.

The primary lesson for George was that love is the only important work in this world. Love people, nature, animals, and creation itself—and to show compassion and generosity.

George took a second doctorate in the psychology of religion. He then became an ordained priest in the Eastern Orthodox Church. The former Russian atheist spent the rest of his career as a pastor at St. Paul United Methodist Church in Baytown, Texas, until he passed away on October 12, 2004.

Dr. Lisa Hurtt

God Has No Religion

At age 37, Lisa Hurtt had it all—a beautiful home, fancy cars, and a boat that would end up turning her idyllic world upside down.

The Accident

On June 19th, 2005, Lisa and her soon to be ex-husband took their boat out on the Lake of the Ozarks with another couple. The day didn't go especially well as Lisa and her husband were constantly fighting.

After a long day, they were trying to get back to the hotel, and the husband of the other couple was driving the boat. The sun had gone down, and they stopped to get their bearings.

As soon as they stopped, a nineteen-year-old driving a cigarette boat ran right over the top of Lisa's boat. Lisa was hit in the head by flying shrapnel, and the boat was cut in half. She fell into the part of the boat that was sinking and drowned. She was dead for twenty-eight minutes.

Her friend awoke Lisa's husband, and they both pulled her on board, but they couldn't resuscitate her. The cigarette boat came back and took them to the shore where the paramedics resuscitated her. They took her to the local hospital to stitch her head up and then airlifted her to Columbia Hospital. The outlook was not good. The doctors told her husband that she might not make it.

She was placed in a medically induced coma for twenty-eight days because her lungs were full of water, and she had a brain injury.

The Near-death Experience

Lisa had no words to describe her experience. We are all limited by our vocabulary and references. Clearly, there are, sounds, colors, and experiences on the other side that we have no words to describe because we've never seen them before. As uncommon as they seem to us in everyday life, they seem to be pretty common in these NDEs, which makes describing them difficult.

Upon impact, Lisa was lifted instantly into the light by two angelic beings. She went into the light and felt a wonderful love, peace, and harmony beyond anything she had experienced. It was a stress- and pain-free existence on the other side.

The angelic beings were tall, had blue eyes, and Mediterranean-colored skin, although they were androgynous. They had long hair and long white robes rather than wings. They were the most beautiful creatures she had ever seen.

They communicated telepathically. She learned that no matter how horrific your accident was, you would feel no pain in that realm.

She was told she would face some hardships when she returned, but that she must not take her own life. She was told to spread the word that there was nothing to fear on the other side. She learned that no one died alone. She had two angelic beings come to her, and she felt that you were stripped of your stress, anger, and ill will toward others when you passed over. All of the stress was released, and you were greeted and guided as you moved into the after-life.

If you had a fight with someone and the last encounter they had with you was negative, if they died they would not carry that anger to the other side. There was only love on the other side.

One message she received stood out. God has no religion. All of the ascended masters played a part in this. God is love, light, and energy. That is God. We are made in God's image. We are made in His image, but most of us do not turn our light on and love others.

Many near-death experience stories include a visit with God or Jesus Christ. However, Lisa felt a connection with every ascended master in history, although she didn't see any human forms except the angelic beings that were more light than form.

The Aftermath

The hardships described to her started with the physical pain of her injuries. Though she was going through a divorce at the same time, her soon to be ex-husband took care of her and helped a great deal in her recovery.

The long-term hardship was the massive medical bills Lisa racked up because she had no health insurance.

She wrote a book, *Divinely Blessed: A Journey of Light*, on how the near-death experience changed her life. She helps people to turn tragedy into transformation and is using the lessons she learned on the other side to help others. She earned a Ph.D. in Holistic Healing and hosts her web radio show, "Simply Spiritual Solutions," on WebTalkRadio.com.

She now uses meditation as her conduit to bring heaven to earth and is teaching meditation to others.

Radio http://webtalkradio.net/simply-spiritual-solutions

Website http://drlisahurtt.com/

Contact Lisa at lisa@drlisahurtt.com

Divinely Blessed: A Journey of Light

Sometimes, It Takes Losing Everything to Gain What Really Matters

The Ripple Effect

She could feel the ligaments tearing and bones breaking as her knees were bent backward.

There's an old joke that I thought of while reading *To Heaven and Back: A Doctor's Extraordinary Account of Her Death, Heaven, Angels and Life Again* by Dr. Mary Neal.

The floodwaters were rising, and a man was on the roof of his house. A man in a rowboat came by to rescue him. The man on the roof said, no, he would wait for God to save him. The floodwaters kept rising, and then a guy in a motorboat came by to rescue the man. The man said he had faith in God and would wait for Him to save him. The floodwaters kept rising. A helicopter then came by to rescue the man. Again, he told the pilot that he had faith in God and would wait for Him to rescue him.

The floodwaters kept rising, and the man

drowned. When he got to heaven, he asked God where he went wrong. He told God that he had faith in God, but God had let him drown. "What more do you want from me?" asked God. "I sent you two boats and a helicopter."

I tell that joke because, as a teenager, Mary Neal was a passenger in a car that went over a ravine. While tumbling down she clearly heard God say to her, "I am with you." She sat back, relaxed, and enjoyed the ride. I see that as the rowboat encounter.

At age 15, she volunteered to help an American missionary couple living in the mountains of central Mexico where they were holding Bible camps and running a rudimentary medical clinic. Mary says she had little interest in their evangelical work and was focused more on the adventure and medical side of the offer. When she asked questions, her hosts suggested she pray for guidance. She thought they were crazy.

Now she says God should get all the credit for

her success and that some patients would not have lived without His intervention. This is like the motorboat offer.

Years later she called out to God to help her and a friend find their way out of a cave and felt the prayer was answered. This is the helicopter corollary.

Even after these extraordinary events, spirituality was still not a driving force in her life. She said that although she was a Christian and believed the Bible was the word of God, her desire for success trumped her desire to move closer to God.

As an adult, she was also skeptical of near-death experiences until she drowned while on vacation in Chile.

The Accident

While paddling down a river on the last day of vacation with her husband, her boat dropped down a waterfall and was pinned between rocks and another boat. She was under water for nearly thirty minutes.

Mary's legs were broken, and she had lung problems after the accident. Her vivid description of feeling both of her knees break and ligaments tearing is an unusual illustration of the expanded clarity many NDEs talk about during the death event and after.

The Near-death Experience

Water engulfed her boat. She made attempts to surface to no avail. Again, she asked for His intervention, not to be saved, but just that His will be done. At that moment, she describes an instant feeling of peace, calm, and of being held and comforted.

Though she never saw Him, she is certain her comforter was Jesus Christ. Mary thought, "How can He be helping me when there are billions of people in need?" It instantly made sense. This is

Jesus Christ, and He is here for all of us.

Jesus took her through a brief life review. Like many life reviews, this was less about judgment and more about the ripple-like changes her actions had on others. Mary describes the profound power of seeing the effects of her words and actions dozens of times removed.

It's interesting that while this was happening, Mary describes still feeling the water around her body, and she was fully aware of her dire situation. She thought about her family and how they would do without her. Once she was assured they would be okay, she got impatient with Jesus to move things along to the next part of the journey.

The Guides

As her soul ascended above the water, Mary was met by a group of radiant spirits and experienced great joy at the feeling she had known them forever. As with virtually all NDEs, communication was non-verbal and instant.

The collective energy was one of celebration or of coming home.

The Light

Mary described the source of brilliant light as a large hall that was pulling them towards the entry. The light enveloped her in an unconditional love far beyond her imagination or experience. She felt all of her questions would be answered in that radiant hall.

At the same time, she was aware that her body had been pulled ashore, and her husband was calling for her. She got annoyed with the pleas for her to return because she wanted so badly to go into the hall.

However, like Carl Jung being prohibited from entering the temple in his near-death experience, Mary was informed that she was not to enter the hall. Her time on earth was not yet up. Despite her protests, she returned to her body.

Conversation with an Angel

Later, lying in the hospital bed, Mary suddenly found herself sitting in a sun-drenched field having a conversation with an angel. She asked many questions of the angel such as "Why do bad things happen to good people?" In the end, the overall message was that God loves everyone. We are all here under His plan. The beggar outside a rich man's office teaches that man compassion. The earth and the humans are truly interconnected. All actions have a reaction.

The Aftermath

Mary struggled to recover from her injuries. In addition to two legs broken at the knees, she had advanced pneumonia and severely inflamed lungs.

Mary feels a mandate to share her near-death experience lessons with others. One of the reasons she was sent back was to help her family deal with the loss of her son Willie some time later. In a strange coincidence, God saved Mary on more than one occasion as a teenager, at age four or five Willie predicted he would never reach age eighteen. One day while roller skiing, Willie was killed instantly when a car hit him. He was ten years old.

After writing her book, Mary has been profiled my many media outlets and is an active speaker on the subject of near-death experiences.

Bio

The author of *To Heaven and Back: A Doctor's Extraordinary Account of Her Death, Heaven, Angels and Life Again*, Mary C. Neal, M.D., is a board-certified orthopedic surgeon, former director of spine surgery at the University of Southern California, and a founding partner of Orthopedic Associates of Jackson Hole, Wyoming. She received her medical degree from the University of California at Los Angeles School of Medicine, where she also trained in general surgery before completing an orthopedic surgery residency at the

University of Southern California.

To Heaven and Back: A Doctor's Extraordinary Account of Her Death, Heaven, Angels, and Life Again: A True Story by Mary C. Neal, M.D.

Joyce Hawkes, Ph.D.

From Science to Spirituality

As an avowed atheist, Joyce had no reference point for heaven or spiritual events like she was experiencing.

In 1976, biophysicist and cell biologist Joyce Hawkes, Ph.D., was housecleaning in Seattle, Washington. She didn't enjoy cleaning and was rushing through the process while vacuuming her bedroom, hallway, and she had nearly finished the living room when a large, heavily framed art piece fell on her head. She dropped to the floor and remained conscious long enough to feel a sharp pain shoot through her body and then she was out cold.

The Near-death Experience

Joyce instantly entered a long tunnel with a

beautiful and welcoming light. At the end of the tunnel, just before the entrance to the lighted area, her dead mother and grandmother stood. They were radiant and in good health, glowing with love, and welcomed her non-verbally. Joyce was overwhelmed to see them.

Since she had no belief in an afterlife, she was astonished to see them. It seemed like they were together for an eternity, and yet she moved on without remorse or sadness into the place where the light was stronger still.

Joyce was amazed at the beauty of what she saw. The sky was a beautiful, luxurious shade of blue. The luminous colors lifted her spirit. Everything was basked in this light. She was standing on a rise with a view of rolling hills lush in greenery. All the colors were beautiful. The flowers glowed as though they were casting their own light.

Joyce enjoyed being immersed in peace and tranquility. She felt a humming of joy from within. She knew she never wanted to leave this place.

She felt totally aware, more aware than she had ever felt before. Joyce walked down the hill into a valley all while enjoying the beautiful sites. She had no sense of time. She felt as if she had been released from the limitations of time and was simply in the present.

Joyce was a staunch atheist. She had no reference point for heaven or spiritual events like she was experiencing. She also had no fear nor did she have a desire to leave.

Without notice, Joyce was whisked back to her living room floor. Her head hurt, and her hair was matted with blood. She didn't seek medical care until her co-workers insisted she see a doctor. His exam revealed a blood clot on her brain, but it didn't require surgery. She was sent home to rest for a few weeks.

Her consciousness expanded and created a new awareness of possible realities. At first, she tried to put her near-death experience out of her mind, but she couldn't dismiss the peace and clarity she had felt. Her near-death experience gave Joyce a new appreciation for life. In fact, she felt that her life was given back to her for a reason, and that reason was to help people.

Post NDE, Joyce noticed her hands emitted heat for some people, and she was able to connect with people through her hands in an extra-sensory manner that she did not have before.

She began to research NDEs and started training with a local healer. She began to meditate daily, and she has experienced a profound calling to healing.

Joyce traveled throughout India, Bali, and the Philippines to study with healers and earned a master's degree in Pastoral Ministry at Seattle University.

Seven years after her near-death experience, she resigned her position and opened a healing practice.

Joyce left science and entered the spiritual

world of healing. To her, healing is about love. God is all about love, and Joyce Hawkes feels she was with God during her near-death experience.

Joyce Whiteley Hawkes, Ph.D., was a biophysicist and cell biologist by training. She completed her doctorate in biophysics at Pennsylvania State University. She was a postdoctoral fellow with the National Institutes of Health before settling in Seattle to work in research for the National Marine Fisheries Service, a part of the National Oceanic and Atmospheric Administration. While there, she was honored with a National Achievement Award for her work.

Mary Jo Rapini

"The Light is Not Impressive."

"Is this the light tunnel my patients describe? If so, I'm not impressed."

The day before Easter Sunday in 2003, psychotherapist Mary Jo Rapini was at Gold's gym lifting weights. She pushed herself to do one more repetition when something popped in her head. It was a scary feeling. It felt as if her body was falling apart. She started sweating profusely, got a massive headache, and her vision was reduced to two little pinholes out the sides. Everything sounded as though she was underwater.

In the ambulance, Mary Jo started to panic. As a nurse, she thought she'd broken her neck. In reality, she had a cerebral aneurysm.

As the pain increased, she said something she'd heard her patients say that she never thought she'd have the strength to say, "God, Your will be done, not mine. I can't handle this. This is too big. Please help me with this."

Even though she was seriously ill, she suddenly felt safe and secure. The ambulance took her to the hospital where she and her husband, a physician, worked. They rushed her to the cat scan machine and discovered her head was full of blood.

She lay in the hospital bed for four days without having surgery, and her conditioned worsened. There were drains in the back of her head to help keep her spinal fluid balanced. When she had a cerebral aneurysm, the drains opened so the blood could drain, but the blood coagulated and clogged up the drains. There was so much blood in Mary Jo's head that they couldn't drain it out. Unless they opened her skull up, her condition would be terminal.

The Near-death Experience

It was during the recovery that she had her near-death experience.

When Mary Jo initially saw the light, she asked

herself, "Is this the light tunnel my patients tell me about? If so, I'm not impressed." But the light got brighter and larger, and she folded into it. It was a warm, loving feeling, and she had no fear.

Mary Jo was moving through the light though she had no sense of having a body. She came out into a magnificent room though she didn't see any walls. It was a brilliant color that defied human language, but she says pink is as close as she can get. The color was loving and accepting.

Mary Jo sensed that God was holding her. She felt a love from God that was not a human love. The love we experience on earth as humans pales in comparison.

God told Mary Jo, much to her disappointment, that she couldn't stay. She protested because what she saw was profoundly beautiful and beyond anything she'd ever experienced. She didn't want to leave. Mary Jo pleaded that she was a good person and treated people well. She worked at the cancer center for only $600 a month. She was on twenty-four-hour call and was always available to help. She soon realized that these were ego-driven reasons that only served her interests. He told her she still had work to do, and that she had not done enough.

God then asked her, "Have you ever loved the way you've been loved here?"

She replied, "No. It's impossible. I'm a human."

In a sort of cosmic chuckle, His reply was, "You can do better."

Then she was back in her bed surrounded by the surgeons, the nurses, and her husband who was crying. He told her she needed surgery and said, "You could die."

She replied, "I can't die. I was just with God and He told me I couldn't die yet." Her husband thought she was hallucinating.

Dying Brings Healing

As someone who has worked with cancer patients for years, Mary Jo had observed countless families praying for their family members. When God didn't heal their bodies, people were disappointed and often angry. Naturally, it seemed unfair for a good person to suffer.

As a result of her near-death experience, Mary Jo believes that the body is limited and, as it's dying, the spirit is being healed. When she was suffering, she felt that process helped to heal her spirit and make her a better person. It prepared her to be used by God in a way that was not possible prior to the illness because of her pride and ego.

Before the illness, she wanted success and material possessions. In the end; none of that matters. Our bodies are limited by the ravages of time. That has nothing to do with God's timeless world. Those wants and desires are part of the limited human world.

The Aftermath

Like many people, Mary Jo found inspiration out

of desperation. Turning your fate over to God's will is incredibly difficult when you are well. When you're facing death or a massive pain, it gets a whole lot easier.

Her near-death experience made Mary Jo a far more spiritual person. She saw people differently. She became more compassionate and less needy for her own wants. She felt complete, which relieved her of want or need.

Mary Jo believes that all of us can have the experience she had. But she doesn't if it is the same for all of us.

Even though she got well, Mary Jo still had to get help with depression. She found the after-life to be so beautiful, and she knew she could never experience that level of love in her earthly existence.

Mary Jo still feels a sense of loneliness. Despite her interaction with God, she sometimes feels rejected by God because He returned her to earth.

It's also frustrating for her to be in the medical field and have people dispute her story as nothing more than a hallucination caused by the aneurysm. More than that, it's the knowledge Mary Jo has that this is not the real world. Your body will end, but your spirit never ends. You're never more alive than you are when you're with God.

Mary Jo was always a spiritual person but felt God was a spirit and could not intervene with us on a human level. She doesn't feel that way now. When she prays to Him, talks to Him, sings to Him, He is with her.

Mary Jo knows God is using her in ways she could have never imagined. She never enjoyed writing yet she's authored two books and writes columns for major newspapers and magazines. She now has a thriving practice as a psychotherapist in Houston. She is a media regular on issues of intimacy and relationships, which is a perfect fit for someone taught directly by God that love is all that matters.

Bio

Mary Jo Rapini, LPC, is a psychotherapist specializing in intimacy, sex, and relationships. Mary Jo maintains a private practice and works with the Methodist Hospital Pelvic Restorative Center as an Intimacy/Sex Psychotherapist and with The Methodist Hospital Weight Management Center. Additionally, she is a renowned lecturer, author, and television personality.

She is the author of *Is God Pink? Dying to Heal*, which describes her near-death experience, and Start Talking, which gives mothers and daughters the tools to start important conversations and strengthen their relationship.

http://www.MaryJoRapini.com

Dr. Ronald Whitaker

He Felt Untold Terror

What did that man hanging on a cross two thousand years ago have to do with me?

In the mid-70s, Ronald Whitaker was a party guy who was out of control with drugs and drinking. He was a well-connected physician with friends in the entertainment business like Hoyt Axton and Ringo Starr.

In late 1974, Axton invited Ronald to attend a TV special in LA. He knew there would be lots of booze and partying, so he was excited to go. After a few days out west, he began to feel ill. He started having severe abdominal pains.

He traveled home and checked into Wadley Hospital in Texarkana in February of 1975. Ronald had acute hemorrhagic necrotic pancreatitis. Rarely, do people live with that disease. You can live with pancreatitis. You can even live with acute pancreatitis, but acute hemorrhagic necrotic pancreatitis is pretty much a death sentence. His potassium, chlorides, and various chemicals were so far out of balance that they had to give him IVs in an attempt to bring them close to normal levels.

At that time, he was a hard-core atheist who was only living for himself. After surgery, he woke up hooked up to a respirator to breathe for him. He couldn't speak, and he had been in a coma, yet he heard doctors and nurses talk about him. They were saying that he did not have much of a chance to live. They said he would never leave the hospital.

He remembered his doctor, Donald Duncan, telling him, "If you have anything to do, right now is the time to do it. If you need anything signed get it done because we don't know how much time you have."

Duncan told Ronald's two sons that he would be dead before the next morning. They didn't expect him to survive. He was aware of this and scared that he was a professed atheist who didn't believe in

God. Ronald believed in the power of the universe because he had seen it. As a physician, he dealt with life and death. He believed in something but had little patience for people who talked to him about God.

For the most part, his peer group of doctors, researchers, and scientists did not believe in God. They did not believe in a supreme being. Everything had to be described by science, which, by its very nature, is lagging in reality.

Ronald worked his way up from being on welfare in Oklahoma to being one of the most powerful men in that part of the country. He said, "It's easy to be an atheist when you're young and successful. It's easy to be an atheist when you've done all of that. But it's very difficult to be an atheist when you're on your deathbed because you begin to think, 'What if these people are right?' "

Ronald recalled that his friend Ron Short had talked to him about Christianity. Ron Short had talked to him about the love of Jesus for five years before Ronald became ill. Ronald debated with Ron, but he liked Ron because Ron did what he said he was going to do. Ron was the only one who Ronald saw that professed to be a Christian and lived as a Christian.

Ronald respected Ron Short. He didn't agree with him, but he respected him. Now that he was on his deathbed, Ron Short was the first person to pop into his head. Ronald started thinking, "What if Ron is right? What if there is a God? How do I get saved? What is saved? What did that man hanging on a cross two thousand years ago have to do with me?" He sent for Ron Short. Ron could not get to the hospital until the next morning, so Ronald had to hold on for one more long nightmarish day.

The Near-death Experience

That night as Ronald was lying in bed, he began to fade away and, as he faded away, he began to go down into darkness. It was so dark. It was like the darkness penetrated his very being, as he left his body. In other near-death experiences, people talked about a light. They talked about floating above their body. They described a feeling of warmth and love. Ronald didn't feel any of that. He felt untold terror.

Ronald was terrified because he knew that if he ever went all the way into the darkness, he would never get back. He knew that, so he fought all night long not to go down again. The hospitals orderlies told him later that he pulled the mattress cover off the mattress. He was fighting to stay until Ron Short arrived to save him.

Ronald's skin began to get cold but not like the cold you felt when you walked outside on a cold evening. It was a bone-chilling cold in his lower extremities that he felt moving up, as each part of his body was going to that dark place that he wanted nothing to do with.

He was leaving his body in the darkness, and he would be in the void again. When he returned to his body, he felt his body thud or plunk down when he returned.

Ronald recalled that as the most terrifying experience that he'd ever encountered. He fought all night long waiting for Ron Short to arrive. When he did, it was around 9 a.m. the next morning.

Ron's first question was, "How much time do you have?"

Ronald's reply was "None."

Ron led Ronald through the Sinner's Prayer. Ron told him that Jesus had died for his sins. He had died for the sins of the world. Ronald didn't quite understand all of that, but he was not questioning anything. As a physician, Ronald was trained in books. Now Ron introduced Ronald to a new book, the Holy Bible.

As Ron led Ronald through the Sinner's Prayer and Ronald repeated the words, he experienced an inner peace, unlike anything he had ever felt. He had searched for that peace in alcohol, in drugs, in women, even in needles.

There was no peace in his life until he accepted Jesus Christ as his Lord and Savior. Though he knew he was hours away from death, he was no longer afraid. People did not survive his illness. Ronald knew this logically because he was a doctor, but he was not God.

Ronald had a full recovery. He takes no medication and is convinced God saved him.

Dr. Eben Alexander

God Help Me!

Dr. Eben Alexander is a neurosurgeon with stellar credentials. He was a resident and research fellow at Brigham and Women's Hospital and Massachusetts General Hospital, and he is certified by the American Board of Neurological Surgery and the American College of Surgeons. He taught at Duke University Medical Center, Brigham and Women's Hospital, Harvard Medical School, University of Massachusetts Medical School, and the University of Virginia Medical.

Ben's father was an academic neurosurgeon and the head of neurosurgery at Wake Forest. He had trained during the WWII years. He learned the craft of neurosurgery in the jungles of New Guinea and the Philippines and, according to Eben; his father got through that as a result of a strong spiritual core.

His father obviously also had a strong scientific sense. You might say Eben's father was of the era when having a strong spiritual, and scientific core were not mutually exclusive. I for one, believe that time is returning.

Despite being raised in a faith-based home and attending a Methodist church, Eben's interest in science challenged his faith early. He recalls having active debates with this sixth grade Sunday school teacher about issues of God, heaven, and science.

After seven years of residency training mainly at Duke, some at Mass General, a fellowship up in Northern England, and fifteen years working at Harvard Medical School on advanced neurosurgery. Alexander worshiped science more than faith.

Another key factor in how he viewed the world was the discovery that he was adopted. His oldest son helped him search for and reach out to his birth mother, but she declined to see him in 2000. Between what he experienced as a neurosurgeon and the rejection of his mother, his faith in a loving

God was crushed.

The Illness

On November 10, 2008 at his home in Lynchburg, Virginia, at age fifty-four, Eben Alexander, M.D., woke at about 4:30 a.m. with severe back pain. What he initially thought was back spasms were actually the rapid onset of a rare form of spinal meningitis, e Coli bacteria. To understand the severity of this strain of spontaneous e coli meningitis has an incidence of around one in ten million per year or less.

His wife Holly thought he was resting, so she left him alone and called some of his colleagues to ask them what to do next. Two hours later, she checked in on him, and he was having a grand mal seizure on the bed.

She called 911, and the first responders couldn't break the seizure. In fact, they took him seizing into the ER even though they'd given him a lot of diazepam and ativan trying to break it.

One of his colleagues, Dr. Laura Potter, said she didn't recognize him when they brought him in. According to her, he looked like someone who was going to die quickly. It took seven orderlies to hold him down for the lumbar puncture.

Interestingly, he was groaning and screaming for an hour or so when, at one point, the faithless Eben Alexander screamed, "God help me!" They were the last words he would speak for seven days.

To get an idea of how severe the meningitis was, the CSF glucose sugar level in the spinal fluid is normally 60 to 80. In somebody with a bad case of meningitis, it might be down to 20. His was down to one!

Furthermore, the onset of the progression of the disease from back pain to severe headache into a coma and a grand mal epileptic seizure is typically within twenty-four hours, yet his was within three to four hours. At that point 90% die. He did not respond for several days to antibiotics, so his odds of survival diminished from 10% down to 2-3% by the end of the week.

Had Eben been his own doctor, he would have told the patient's family that the odds of a neurological recovery were very limited. If he survived, he would probably spend the rest of his life in a nursing home.

As if that was not enough to garner this book's "miracle recovery honors," it is highly unusual for patients lucky enough to survive such an onslaught to have any memory at all of the experience. Eben remembered everything.

Meningitis works to destroy the neocortex, the outer surface of the brain, which is the part that makes us human. This is a major fact in this near-death experience. His neocortex was shut down. Consciousness had to operate outside of the neocortex.

The Near-death Experience

In an uncharacteristic opening NDE scene, Eben first recalls "a visible darkness." He was within a blurry type of "dirty Jell-O" that was suffocating. At the same time, he felt a rhythmic pulsing or pounding in the air and land.

Eben was unaware of having a body. In fact, he was unaware of language, emotion, logic, memories, family, even his name. He felt as though he had regressed back to the beginning of time but like most near-death experiences, time doesn't exist.

Being there was all he knew. He was simply in the present with no knowledge of past or future.

The Revealing

As Eben's awareness expanded, he saw or sensed root-like growths around him. He likens the experience to being a worm in the ground tangled with roots and growth. Later he called this the Realm of the Earthworms' Eye View.

As he became more uncomfortable in this realm of worms, repulsive animal faces began to emerge from the mud, and muck emitting pained sounds and re-submerging. Some sounds seemed like ancient chants.

He began to experience the smell, and it was not a pleasant odor. He described it as "biological death."

Though his anxiety increased as his awareness of his macabre surroundings increased, he had no idea where to go or what to do about it.

The Light

A pure white light, tinged in gold, descended accompanied by "the richest, most complex, most beautiful piece of music you've ever heard."

Eben perceived an opening in the light and rapidly entered a world totally the opposite of what he had been experiencing. He described it as the strangest and most beautiful world he'd ever seen.

Familiarly, he cites a lack of words powerful enough to describe what he saw and experienced.

The Landscape

Eben describes earth that is not quite like our earth. He saw adults, children, even dogs, all playing, singing, running, and jumping. Most of all, he felt the place was completely real, indeed, "hyper-real." People wore simple peasant-like clothes that had pleasant, warm colors.

The Guide

Eben noticed a beautiful girl and realized they were riding on the wing of a butterfly. They spoke without speaking. The message was essentially, "You are loved. You have nothing to fear. You can do no wrong here." For Eben, the effect was instant relief.

She said that they would teach him, but he must return. Eben had no idea where he was from.

The Angels

He described beautiful winged shimmering orbs soaring across the sky that he sensed were higher entities.

Eben described hearing and seeing as a blended experience. He was hearing the beauty and seeing the music. It seemed as though he became part of everything he saw and heard.

The wisdom of the divine came to him in the form of a beautiful warm wind. His questions were answered "instantly in an explosion of light, color, love, and beauty." The answers were nonverbal.

Interestingly, Eben used the pronoun "Om" for God. While Om is a mantra used in Buddhist meditation, he associates Om with omniscient and omnipotent.

The Om told him love was at the center of all of the universes, and there were many. Evil is required for us to have free will.

The Aftermath

Eben describes his near-death experience in some ways as a "perfect storm" of near-death experiences. As a practicing neurosurgeon with decades of research and hands-on work in the operating room, he was in a much-better-than-average position to judge the experience and its implications.

Before his near-death experience, Eben would have said the brain caused any such experience. The brain creates consciousness is the theory for materialistic thinkers and atheists. Kill the brain and the consciousness dies.

After his near-death experience, Eben said the implications were beyond description. His experience showed him that the death of the brain and body are not the end of consciousness. The human experience continues after death. He states that the after-life is under the "gaze of God who loves and cares about each of us and about where the universe itself and all the beings within it are ultimately going."

Eben is convinced his near-death experience is impossible to explain through typical neuroscience. If anyone is qualified to know, it's Eben Alexander, M.D.

Eben Alexander M.D. Official Website and Amazon Page

http://www.LifeBeyondDeath.net

Proof of Heaven: A Neurosurgeon's Journey into the Afterlife

In the End

In reflection, it's interesting that despite a religious undercurrent to these amazing stories, no religion was specifically mentioned by any of the guides. I believe that the message is that love is more important than ritual.

Religion helps humans to organize and interact under a common belief, but neither God nor His Son created religion. Man created religion and, typical of man, there will always be the top third, middle third, and bottom third of religions that accurately reflect their deities intentions and serve their followers.

The people in this book were not met at the gate and asked for their membership card. Love was the ultimate VIP entry, yet they were accepted and loved even though they did not have the "card."

Yes, some were closer to God than others, but each visit was clearly a cosmic teaching moment rather than a scolding for past deeds.

Carl Jung's near-death experience had a black

Hindu priest that he never interacted with, much to his disappointment. That is the only naming of a religion that was part of any near-death experience in this book. The near-death experience seems to be an infinitely spiritual experience but not specifically religion centered.

When Jung wrote about his near-death experience in 1944, he described it as a journey to meet the self and the Divine. He cautioned that modern humans rely too heavily on science and logic, and they would benefit from integrating spirituality and appreciation of the unconscious realm into their lives.

I'm sure he finally made it into that temple and that the Hindu priest told him where he fit in the historical nexus.

The most concrete religious encounter was Ronald Whitaker being saved at the last hour by Ron Short, which is a remarkable testimony considering Ronald had a fatal illness.

George Ritchey had a direct experience with

Jesus that changed his life. "Stand at attention soldier!" I could just see his eyes bug out and jumping to his feet. George was shown a 50/50 possibility, and he wanted nothing to do with the darker option. He spent years teaching that to others.

No doubt, your history with a certain religion, or lack of, might influence what you experience during one of these episodes.

Anthony Cicoria's experience with God led him to believe in a reincarnation process more similar to Buddhism than Christianity. That, plus his fascinating newly found talent in classical music, is a great indicator of the positive effects of a near-death experience.

It's no surprise then that Anthony started practicing meditation. Buddhists describe meditation as a path to Nirvana. A number of our subjects took to mediation after their NDE. In addition to Anthony, Mary Jo Rapini, Lisa Hurrt, and Eben Alexander have begun to meditate to try to reconnect on some level with the other side. For them, meditation is the best path of connection. If these stories were all about religions, wouldn't you expect them all to say they have had more success with prayer? Again, I think the connection is what matters; the technique is secondary.

How about the fact that both George Ritchy and Mary Jo Rapini were asked, "Have you ever loved the way you've been loved here?" They both had nearly identical answers, "How, we're just human?" Though I suspect Mary Jo may have added, "I can learn that real fast if you would just let me stay!"

I found the story of George Rodonaia, Russian atheist, and scientist, especially interesting. He was run over by the KGB in Georgia, spent three days dead in the morgue, and then he was returned to his body just in time to feel the scalpel slice into his stomach. Welcome back, George!

When you think of a staunch atheist, it doesn't get more hardline that a communist era scientist in Russia-dominated Georgia. To go from that belief to becoming an ordained priest and serve as a pastor in Baytown, Texas—talk about a lifestyle change. I wonder if he started saying, "Howdy" and "ya'll" with a Russian accent.

Atheists George Rodonaia, Eben Alexander, and Ronald Whitaker all started their near-death experiences in the dark. George used the power of positive thinking to rise out. Eben used a slowly emerging awareness to reach out. Ron Whitaker held on to life just long enough to get saved and healed in an amazing one-two punch.

Isn't it ironic how Mary Neal was saved more than once, and how her son Willie predicted his death and it happened? It was as though God had to show her that Willie was going to be all right. I have no idea how much comfort that gave her, but I hope it was a lot.

I love the playful way she described hurrying up Jesus to move things along. That lady has spunk.

Joyce Hawkes was a self-described atheist, yet she didn't get the dark treatment. She had a beautiful, albeit short, near-death experience that served as a calling to become a healer, which is way, way out there for a cell biologist. Her experience gifted her with hands that seem to be able to emit heat to some people and help her intuitively know what is going on with their ailment. It's a wonderful gift and, not to be corny, in the right hands.

The superstar of NDErs has to be Eben Alexander. His story has captivated the country and frustrated his skeptics. The best the skeptics can offer is that Dr. Alexander is only a lowly neurosurgeon and NOT a neuroscientist. Who hangs out with these people? Dr. Alexander has stellar creds, and I don't need to repeat them here ... Okay, he taught neurosurgery for fifteen years at this backwoods little school called HARVARD UNIVERSITY! There, that felt good.

In the end, I believe that there is far more going on in our dimensions than we can ever hope to grasp or imagine in this earthly existence.

As I mentioned in the introduction, I'm going to paraphrase Dr. Sam Parnia, who is a well-known NDE researcher. He said if you told someone two hundred years ago that we'd have the technology to send a human to the moon and bring them back to tell about; most people would think you were crazy. We may be getting close to the place where, under clinical conditions, we can send one into the after-life and safely bring them back to tell us all about the experience.

I think we may be doing that already.

About The Author

Tampa Bay, FL resident, John Graden is the author of many books on personal development, martial arts, marketing, and near death experiences.

He is an inductee to the Self-Publishers Hall of Fame and the Million Dollar Author Club. His many media appearances include "The Dr. Oz Show," a cover story on the "Wall Street Journal", and his book "The Impostor Syndrome" was on the cover of "Publishers Weekly."

His websites include:

http://JohnGraden.com"

http://GenerateMoreLeads.com"

http://NDEBook.com"

http://MartialArtsTeachers.com"

http://SelfDefenseBusiness.com

Made in the USA
San Bernardino,
CA